BACK POCKET

Adventure

Karl Rohnke & Jim Grout

ILLUSTRATED BY ANNA DEWDNEY

Project Adventure, Inc.

Published in conjunction with
Simon & Schuster Custom Publishing

SIMON & SCHUSTER
CUSTOM PUBLISHING

A special thanks to Anna Dewdney for her wonderful illustrations that capture the child-like thrill of playing and the PA Covington office and Vermont Academy for some last-minute photos with their students and staff.

Printed in the United States of America

Please visit our website at www.sscp.com

10 9 8 7 6 5 4 3 2 1

ISBN 0-536-01419-1

BA 98508

SIMON & SCHUSTER CUSTOM PUBLISHING
Simon & Schuster Education Group
160 Gould Street/Needham Heights, MA 02494

Contents

Preface   5

What's Adventure Education Got To Do
*   with My Back Pocket?*   9

Facilitation Tips   13

Activities

7-11   23
Air Traffic Controller   25
Back to Back   29
Belly Up   31
Como Está Usted   33
Competition Line-Up   36
Corporal Golf   38
Cyclops Tag   41
Deeply Rooted   44
Figaro, Figaro, Figaro!   47
Fun-Con-Nada   50
Go To and Touch Blue   52

Contents

Great to See You 55

Grouplets 57

Have You Never...? 58

Humpty Histrionics 61

I'm Going on a Trip 63

Map Making 65

Me Too aka The Chosen Few 67

Name of the Game 68

Name Roulette 70

Out of Kilter 72

Pairing Up Ideas 74

Phizz, Splot, Grooby 76

Pixillated Proverbs 78

Poignant Pictures 83

Poseur 86

Robart Tag 87

Sweet Harmony 90

Take Me To Your Leader 92

Tic-Tac-Toe—Live! 94

Weird Walkin' 96

Welded Ankles 98

Wham Sam Sam 100

Preface

Seems like I've been doing this one-day game and initiative stuff since they invented dirt, including years of racing to and through various airports and school parking lots, hauling and dragging a large green canvas bag chock-a-block full of toys, Ice Breaker items, game paraphernalia and miscellaneous creativity stimulators, all in the name of proper props and functional facilitation. BUT, the real reason for hauling around that humongous bag was—I *needed* those props. The quantity of game goodies guaranteed that I had enough to fill the day and would never get caught without something to do. (Feel the angst?)

About a year ago I was scheduled to present a half-day workshop with a conference group in downtown some-where. I arrived at the hotel early and found the sterile room where the presentation was scheduled. "Presentation" in this context means to turn the folks on to Adventure program-ming via a series of hands-on experiential activities that are atypical enough to allow participation without fear-of-failure. Thus, the bag of tricks—my professional comfy object.

With about half an hour 'til show time, I plopped my bag at the door and bopped down to the local Starbucks for a double latté, watched people for awhile, then casually wandered back to the assigned venue. My bag was gone!

Not just misplaced, actually ripped off... I hope the thief likes bits of rope, squeaky toys and balloons.

No problem, I'm a professional. AAArgh! WHAT AM I GOING TO DO WITH SIXTY PEOPLE FOR FOUR HOURS WITHOUT PROPS? Stranded, propless in a strange city, not a toy or hardware store near enough to help. The only movable objects in the room were a lectern, a jug of water and some fake flowers. Help! The people are rapidly collecting... looking at me... anticipating... wondering...

"OK folks, it's time to get experiential. Line up in a circle, and let's get started."

The four hours went by without a hitch as I somewhat seamlessly presented a series of propless experiences. I was amazed, not so much at myself for pulling it off, but with the fact that for years I had been hauling around a cumbersome bag of nonessential props. Don't get me wrong, the green bag-of-tricks includes some great toys that stimulate fun, participation and a giddy sense of child-like glee. I'd hate to entirely give up those *tools*, but there's a remarkable sense of facilitating freedom available by collecting and practicing experiential-based activities that do not require props—games and initiatives that can literally be pulled out of your back pocket; i.e., your mind.

Here's a small book suggesting minimal travel luggage for Jim and I, and maximum creative use for you. Come on along and let's see what we can do with nothing. — *KER*

Going Propless: Three Rationals

Number One

Some years ago I recall saying to a fellow staff member, "I think the best thing to encourage your creativity would be if you went to Seattle to do a job and I sent your game bag to Indianapolis." I didn't intend the comment disparagingly but rather to challenge what I perceived to be his undo reliance on "the bag." At the time I was beginning to feel that Adventure was getting too prescriptive and predictable based upon the stuff you brought to the job. You know, "who cares what the group needs, I've got to do *Keypunch*, it's on the agenda." Actually, I've experienced this dilemma more than once over the years and was probably unfairly projecting some of my own frustration when I made the above suggestion to my Adventure friend.

Number Two

On another occasion I was in the Atlanta airport for the first time and hauling along my large green PA game bag. I arrived in Concourse D, which is only about twelve miles from the baggage claim. (I know you're wondering why am I headed to baggage claim when I'm already hauling baggage, or why didn't I just ship the green monster in the first place... great questions.) Anyway, I leave Concourse D and begin the trek to baggage claim. It's after midnight, I'm tired, hot and hungry and unclear about where I'm trying to go. Early on, I notice a subway to my right. I foolishly assume that this subway probably heads into downtown Atlanta. Given the late hour and my confusion about its likely destination, I decide it would be unwise to board and continue my trek for at least another twelve miles. After 30+ minutes, I arrive at the baggage claim immeasurably tireder, hotter and hungrier than I was back at Concourse D. Also massively disappointed in myself when I see the "subway to Atlanta" depositing passengers neatly at the entrance to the baggage claim. I curse myself and I curse the green bag.

Number Three

Last winter, I'm headed to Iowa to do a *QuickSilver* Day at Iowa State hosted by Lauren Petrie. Thanks for having us Lauren, you were a great host. Anyway, I arrive in Iowa, again after midnight. My green bag (shipped this time) does not. I inquire at the Delta lost luggage desk when I might expect its return. "Well, there are no more flights tonight and the first one out of Rapid City in the morning gets your bag here about 11:00 AM." I recall my comment mentioned in Rationale #1 and determine that fate has brought this dilemma upon me. I *did* panic slightly.

The next morning I asked Lauren to round up whatever Adventure paraphernalia she might have. She didn't have much. As I recall we did activities until about 1:00 PM using virtually no props. For the remainder of the afternoon I improvised with whatever Lauren had on hand. The day went great, and I felt exhilarated at having engaged the troops with less rather than more. When I arrived back at the motel, the desk clerk greeted me with a very friendly Iowa welcome and said, "Mr. Grout, you'll be happy to know your bag has arrived." She looked so pleased. I couldn't begin to tell her she was looking at a man who no longer needed a *bag*.

Summary

These three experiences have brought me down the road less traveled, the road less encumbered, the road to propless bliss. Certainly not all the time because there are some great props in those bags and boxes (Hey, we sell the stuff after all.), but it's nice to know that your creativity can prevail, your load can be lighter and people will still laugh and learn when you present them with less not more.

So, we hope that this little book will bring you to *No Props? No Problem*. If nothing else, it's easier to carry… just stuff it in your back pocket. — *Jim Grout*

What's Adventure Education Got To Do with My Back Pocket?

Silver Bullet, *QuickSilver* and *Back Pocket* days = 8 hours of engineered fun and games mixed with some pedagogic rationale. Participants give up a day of their time, usually a day's wages, and pay to attend. Why? What's the attraction?

Something good happens based on the curriculum content of that training day. I'm about to suggest what's *good*, but don't settle in for a long read; this stuff's simple, and the simplicity underlines its effectiveness.

Brief rhetorical caveat: If you read this and don't combine the text with a most essential ingredient—EXPERIENCE— you miss the essence of what we're suggesting. Not twenty years of vicarious experience, I'm talking about hands-on doing these things, trying this stuff. Honestly, you have to experience what we call Adventure Programming to appreciate it's power—power to change: lives, ideas, ways of thinking, relationships, YOU!

Your potential players—students, workshop participants, campers, whomever—are in an institutional groove. Their recreation choices have been predetermined by an out-dated physical education approach (being hammered with a win/lose philosophy), to the extent that game situations are almost invariably competitive. The trust level they anticipate while *playing* with others is about nil, because they were never taught how to play.

It's disappointing how electronic gizmos have come to be considered playthings—TV, game boys, Sega, game arcades... And now, because two-dimensional "Kombat" isn't real enough, we are offered virtual reality, affording the electronic capability of being able to buy whatever reality suits your two dimensional mood. But, the argument goes, a player's eye/hand coordination becomes much enhanced. Great...

Enough soap boxing... Based on over 25 years experience in this fledgling field, here's a few reasons why experiential education works.

- **Communication** happens. When you provide an encounter, a problem-solving situation that people are intrigued by and respond to, they begin to talk. After a substantial amount of trial and error, players discover that to experience a level of satisfying play, they must also listen. If the situation presented captures a sense of reality (no matter how fabricated it really is), and the challenge is essentially real, they will talk and they will listen—communication happens

- **Cooperation** occurs. What a horrendously over-worked, over-used concept. Mentioning cooperation to a divergent group is like providing a snooze button for a narcoleptic. But when cooperation happens, things happen, results occur. Present an attractive challenge. Do or do not, allow no equivocation. Action is inevitable, and to achieve the goal, cooperation becomes key. Without you, without me, we remain as one, standing at the base of *The Wall* wondering what's on the other side.

- Without **Trust,** communication and cooperation are just two C words that look good on a proposal. Shared experiences together build trust, and it grows, slowly... so slowly. Trust is based on respect and consistency. Fear must be overcome; fear of failure, emotional discomfort, physical pain. Fear diminishes as trust builds. But protect it, nurture every forward failure, because trust that took weeks to establish can be dashed in seconds.

- **FUN,** fun, FUN, Fun, fun, fun, FUN, fun, FUN—If what you present isn't enjoyable, people will not come back willingly to experience more of whatever you have to offer. This is the easiest concept to accept and often the most difficult to implement. Our society pays lip service to the efficacy of adult play, but when the bottom-line parental/scholastic/corporate chips are down, the concept of play slips to pejorative. Rediscovering the capacity for play can be an extremely powerful experience. (It was tempting to write *productive play* in the last sentence but that's not FUN.)

Facilitation Tips

Don't take yourself and what you're presenting too seriously. We don't expect you to change your approach to teaching or philosophical outlook by offering a few tips, but… who really cares if someone runs out of bounds from time to time, or tweaks the rules to fit the occasion? It's the level of participation that's significant; i.e., the percentage of people willing to play. The concept of play is essential, the game is just a vehicle—seriously. You want to collect more than $200 for passing GO? You got it.

Humor makes the program. If you don't regularly infuse your approach, presentation and evaluation with some smidgen of humor, don't anticipate enthusiastic participant response. This does not mean that you have to wear a red clown's nose or teach a la Sesame Street. The best humor comes from subtly spontaneous situations and the participants themselves.

Explain the game's structure and rules as simply and clearly as possible, and do it in a style that encourages participation, playfulness, fantasy and fun. You are the gamemaster. If you aren't, become one. (Gamemasters are self-certified.)

When explaining rules, set a tone indicating that rules should be followed only as long as the group wants to follow them. Be open to rule changes. Avoid anarchy, promote communication and creativity.

Change the rules of whatever you are doing to fit the situation. Rules in this context are not made to be written down or consistently reinforced. Consider these three profound suggestions:

1. If the group likes a certain rule and following that rule creates more fun, keep it.
2. If the group doesn't like a rule, play without it.
3. Remaining personally out of context helps.

Also, try rule variations from time to time to see how the group responds. Most people have been taught to adhere to rules, "or else," so be aware that there's bound to be some resistance when you suggest making third base first base, and running counterclockwise (Aussie Rules) or whether you strike the boulard or not. See, tweaking the game vocabulary helps too.

Encourage the group, through participation, to begin to understand the value of shared stupidity. Demonstrate the games with appropriately outrageous or foolish words and actions, then encourage your players to join you. You need to play the fool first, but be a cool-fool, not a stupid one.

Footballs, basketballs and baseballs are not good play objects. Oh they're fine for the established sports whose name they represent, but there's bounteous balls for pick-up games that function much better than foot/basket/baseballs. (Ref. boulard above.)

If you haul out a classic ball (football, say) you can expect a predictable mind set (or gut set) from your assembled players. "All right!, let's make some contact!" Or, "Aarrgh, I'm going to get killed again." Some can't wait to play, some cringe at the thought and some just participate because they've been told to.

Use balloons, rubber chickens, deck tennis rings, fleece balls, beach balls, soft squeaky toys—things different and fun; things that might make you smile; things not associated with previous failures or embarrassments.

Use different and unique names for the games you play and the play objects—names that are fun to say. If the students ask, "What are we going to do today?" and you say, "Volleyball," that's a pretty good indication of what the class will be doing; i.e., predictable. Then it's either, "Yippee!" or "Oh, no!" or "Who cares?" Rather indicate, "Today we'll play *Italian Golf*, or maybe try a fast round of *Cucaracha*." Have you played *Cucaracha?* Have your students? Is there a chance they might be intrigued by something new?

- Establish a comfortable relationship with the participants right away; talk, share, compare, smile, be at ease.

- Create an atmosphere that is an *invitation to learn*.

- Extend an obvious, well heard and open welcome to all new (late) arrivers.

- Establish yourself as a player as well as a leader right from the get-go. Personalize the games with your person.

- Begin with games that include movement and have few, easily explained rules. Examples: *Moon Ball*, *Impulse*, *PDQ* tricks.

- Let the players stretch their bodies and their feelings sloooowly at first; no running, no competition, no contest—yet.

- Combine description with demonstration, facial gymnastics and no-holds histrionics. Don't lecture!

- After a period of play, ask for feedback about the game. If a particular comment suggests an interesting variation, use that spark of creativity as an opportunity to empower the participants, allowing the group to take charge of the game.

- Always offer choices. A coerced player is no longer a player.

- Before a physically active game, point out areas that require a safety mind-set; e.g., big people watching out for little people (not necessarily just physical size), fend off rather than knock down.

- Know the rules well enough to help the group change them.

- If you invent a game or initiative activity, congratulations, but do not claim the game as yours. "A good idea doesn't care who has it." Share… share… share.

Is this humerus? Not exactly. Humerus is actually a large bone of the upper arm, located immediately distal to the scapula, or proximal to the radius and ulna, depending on where you're coming from. It's a fairly funny-bone, but not in the same class as ribs, which are prone to tickle.

A Second Look at Challenge by Choice & Full Value Contract

Hold it! Don't turn the page just yet. If these two terms are familiar to you, we're sure you're probably ready to move on, fully believing that nothing new could be said about them. But guess what? Recent studies have shown that both of these concepts can be easily misconstrued, manifesting the MISSES* syndrome, which has been known to cause value judgments in otherwise healthy individuals.

Are you still reading? Good, we've got your attention. Now, here's the real update on these two concepts.

Challenge by Choice

The comment we most frequently hear about efforts to instill this concept with students is, "I explained Challenge by Choice to my students and now many of them decide,

---

* MISSES: Misapprehension, misunderstanding, misinterpretation, miscomprehension

upon hearing the description of an activity, game or initiative that we're going to do, that their choice is to *not* participate."

Whoops, let's back up. The original intent (Karl Rohnke circa 1974) of Challenge by Choice was to offer participants:

■ A chance to try potentially difficult challenges in an atmosphere of support and caring.

■ The opportunity to "back off" when performance pressures or self-doubt become too strong, knowing that an opportunity for a future attempt will always be available.

■ A chance to try difficult tasks, recognizing that the attempt is more significant than performance results.

■ Respect for individual ideas and choices.

It would appear that what started as a concept to bring people to a point of challenge—where they felt faced with difficulty, stress, self-doubt or pressure and thereby needed to make a choice—has somehow come to be interpreted as offering the choice first and the challenge second. If taking risks leads to growth, then it's important to assure that challenge occurs, and that the challenge is not a demand, rather an invitation to risk in a supportive atmosphere that assigns more significance to an attempt than the level of performance.

So what do you do?

Invite

Offer Fun

Engage

Challenge!

Full Value Contract (Commitment)

There are numerous versions of the Full Value Contract extant in the Adventure world today. This is not a right or wrong situation, just variations on a theme. Which is as it should be, because each group defines itself differently. Also, the group's needs around how they want *to be together* are predictably different.

Therein lies the challenge. Any prescribed contract that *requires* participants to commit to behavior norms before the group has gotten a chance to discover one another represents a dictated series of guidelines by definition; certain to be ignored.

When we have heard back from folks in the field that they are having difficulty getting buy-in from their students regarding the Full Value Contract, the problem seems to lie in the fact that "a particular version" of FVC is being forced upon the group as opposed to the group creating its own version after spending a period of time together.

When time doesn't allow for creating a contract, a version we like that seems to be simple and clear is:

- Participate
- Work Together
- Share Opinions & Feelings
- No Put Downs
- Be Safe
- Have fun

An activity such as *The Being* has proven to be an invaluable tool for achieving group ownership of behavior and defining how a group wants to be together.

Hey, wait a minute. We just said don't use a prescriptive approach to the FVC and then we went ahead and gave you one. Pardon our boldness. Well, forget you ever saw this. Don't use it!

The Being

One of the activities we use frequently to work with our groups on the Full Value Contract is called The Being. The Being is a large outline of a person or object that the group picks to symbolize itself. It could be a person, animal, tree, anything at all. Give the group an old sheet or large piece of newsprint or poster board and have them draw the outline of the object they have selected to represent them. If they've decided to use a participant, ask someone to volunteer to lie down on the sheet or newsprint so that the group can trace the outline of their body. Once that's done, ask the group to brainstorm a list of the positive behaviors they want the group to maintain—listening, caring, supporting, cooperating, respecting opinions—and write them down inside the drawing. Then ask the group to think of behaviors that distract them or keep them from meeting these positive behavioral goals—ignoring new ideas, goofing off, devaluing—and write those down outside the drawing.

You can come back to your Being whenever you want, adding behaviors as they come up or simply referring to it and asking if everyone feels that the group's guidelines are being adhered to and respected.

ACTIVITIES

ACTIVITIES

7-11

Fingers. You like finger games? Well, here's one anyway.

■ Play

Three people (which happens to be a troika) stand facing one another, as troikas are wont to do.

One of the players says, "One, two, three, SHOOT." On SHOOT, all three players throw out as many fingers (0–5) on one hand as they deem necessary to come up with a solution, which is: To achieve the number 7; i.e., the total

number of fingers being spontaneously exhibited. Any other digital total is wrong and the process must be repeated until 7 is achieved.

Obviously talking or sharing signals is not allowed.

Since there is absolutely no skill involved, the number of SHOOT times necessary to reach 7 will vary from the first time to many more than that. The happy circumstance develops that no one seems to care how many times it takes, being taken up in the laughter and ludicrousness of what's happening.

Variation

If players enjoy trying to reach 7, suggest that they use both hands and try to achieve 11. Same rules and procedure, but it takes longer.

Tidbit of Simplicity

*Order and simplification
are the first steps toward
mastery of a subject.*

—Thomas Mann

Air Traffic Controller

Nope, this isn't about a rappel device. This trust activity is a no prop, full field extravaganza; all you need is people and space to move, like a well-turfed field.

It came to mind as the result of missing a flight at the Salt Lake City airport. It's not like I wasn't paying attention, I just didn't hear the announcement. When I looked up from the paper I was reading (USA Today weather page) there was no one sitting near me. Drawing on my years of travel experience and a keen sense of where I'm not, my ISU* sensors were screaming that something was not right. My plane (their plane) had left about three minutes ago as I was checking out the color temperature contours over the Mid-West.

I immediately complained to the beleaguered desk attendant that since I was a frequent, frequent flyer that someone should have come over and invited me to board at my leisure, but I was obviously in the wrong, and my specious complaint faded to a "why me…" whine. I had been sitting patiently for an hour and now I had an additional three hours tacked on as a penalty for not listening to the barely audible garbled monotone of:

"…flight5272tochicagowillboardassoonasyouarenotlistening."

* ISU — I Screwed Up

Air Traffic Controller

With 180 minutes of Starbucks, TCBY (This Can't Be
Yogurt), and regular recorded admonitions to "watch my
luggage" staring me in the face, I bolted for any automatic
door (sliding or rotary, I was desperate) that would let me
breathe real air.

Bags in hand, I climbed the stairs to the top of the adjacent
open-air parking garage and found a spot to sit that offered a
view, cooling breezes, and minimal auto exhaust. I remember
thinking to myself, "How come I don't have to pay for this?"

Like most kids, I like to watch planes take off. Really, how
can something that big stay up? The jets were leaving the
ground at regular intervals; every two minutes, I timed them.
As I watched the planes zoom off I imagined what it must
be like in the control tower, having to keep up with all the
takeoffs and landings that were taking place, and a game
came to mind...

■ Play

Throw a couple shirts or hats on the ground about 6 feet
apart. This careful positioning represents the aircraft carrier
launch area.

Participants then line up in pairs in a double column behind
and perpendicular to the launching shirts. (Check out the
illustration.)

One member of the pair takes on the role of aircraft, the other
functions as pilot. The aircraft has no sensing devices (eyes
closed) and the pilot directs the craft with verbal commands
only; i.e., no physical contact, unless a crash is imminent.

As the flight pair moves onto the field (you will be launching
a new pair about every five seconds), the pilot maneuvers

26

his/her plane as carefully or dramatically as the situation and trust level allow.

As more and more pairs make their way onto and around the field, the opportunity for excitement (and crashes) increase. This exercise is supposed to build trust; emphasize that concept with the participants before granting their pilot's licenses. All planes have been equipped with safety bumpers. These bumpers (hands up at chest level, palms facing out) should be up and in use at all altitudes.

Air Traffic Controller

After all the planes have been launched, begin the process of bringing the planes and pilots back to the deck of the aircraft (which will, of course, have moved by this time — reposition the shirts to another part of the field). To bring them back, call out the pilot or the plane's name, not necessarily in their launch sequence.

The idea is to "land" the pairs in rapid succession (through the small entrance outlined by the shirts) so that the pilots have to think and react quickly. After all the planes are safely "on deck," ask the partners to switch roles and prepare again for take off.

Encourage the planes to make lots of plane-like noises while zooming around the field. A developing airborne cacophony adds to the intensity of flight response, and more pragmatically allows the planes to hear who they are about to collide with.

Just one more thing...

If you are imagining all the things that could go wrong (see * ISU syndrome), good thinking. Know your group and their current capacity for trust before presenting this free-form exercise. Air Traffic Controller is an example of an activity that could be sequenced out of sequence.

BACK TO BACK

I'm sure that I wrote about this activity at some time in some other book, but I just spent longer looking for it than I should have. Anyway, it's not the activity that I'm interested in passing along, but a revelation about the activity that was passed along to me. This is one to get the creativity flowing.

■ Play

There you are on a warm summer workshop day, leaning back-to-back against your partner, taking a brief break from the frenetic presentation of lactic acid games, perhaps vaguely wondering what your partner is doing.

Your partner is doing what you should already have started, changing five identifiable things on your person.

When you turn to face one another, after a few minutes of preparation time, each person of the duo tells their partner what they think is different from what they observed previously.

Pretty straight forward, mildly interesting but not much of a challenge. OK, get back-to-back again and this time change ten things. Hmmm, the challenge has definitely escalated.

OK, time's up, check out what bizarre creative changes your partner has come up with. Glasses on upside down? Shoes on backward? Watch on the other wrist? A Ginkgo leaf stuck up their nose? But you did find ten observable things to change.

Nice going. Assume the dorsal/dorsal positioning once again and this time change/find another ten.

Just one more thing...

"Come on... I don't have anything left to change, and I've run out of props." When this activity was presented to me I voiced that exact sentiment. I felt put upon to try and come up with even one more changeable item. I was blown away during the debrief when the facilitator held up his hand and pulled in one finger after another until all ten tucked digits resulted in two fists—ten changes. I had nestled into the less-than-creative comfort of my performance box. I had reacted vertically while lateral was crying to be seen. I could change anything; gestures, positioning, emotion... The changes available to me and my partner were infinite. WOW! Was I impressed. Now it's your turn to impress someone.

Tidbit of Simplicity

There is no greatness where there is not simplicity.

— Tolstoi

Belly Up

Have you ever seen horseshoe crabs washed up on shore? It's a bit of a pitiful site in that they often get flipped over by the tide, "belly up," unable to right themselves. As the tide goes out, there they are stranded in the littoral zone awaiting the next tide or a contingent of "Save The Crabs" minded people to extricate them from an established fate.

Well in this game version of crab life, you've got no returning tide to save you, only good intentioned crab lovers fighting against all odds. This is a group initiative in which the group will have several attempts to improve their time and "save the crabs."

■ Play

Have a group of ten plus (the more the better) players lie down on their bellies, then bend their legs up behind them and grab their feet. Do this in an undefined playing area, as in crabs spread out all along the beachfront (grass field in this case). Then establish a low water mark (a.k.a. piece of rope) about thirty feet away from the group.

Establish one player as the "Crab Champion" and have him/ her join the others in the backward bent prone position. On a starting signal of "Save the Crabs!" chanted in unison by all crabs, the object is for folks to right themselves;

Belly Up

i.e., maneuver onto their backs without letting go of their feet, and run to the safety of the low-water mark. However, none of this action may begin, until the designated "Crab Champion" has righted him/herself, at which time all crabs in trouble commence wriggling and emitting piteous cries of pain, particularly if they are not limber and supple of body. Since, genetically, age has everything to do with a crabs ability to right itself, the Champion, (only the Champion) can assist any struggling crabs by giving them a little nudge in the turning process.

The clock starts with "Save the Crabs" and stops when the last person has reached the safety of the low water mark (rope). Obviously operating in a Crustacean mind-set (often referred to as ganglion groping), all movement toward the low tide mark must be accomplished crab-style (prone orientation with only hand and foot contact with the turf). Any crab having trouble with this method of locomotion can receive crab-aid from any other crabby crustacean available. What does that involve? S'up to you as king of the crabs.

As when attempting any initiative, allow some strategy time between attempts. Times will vary greatly depending upon the age and flexibility of the crabs (thirteen-year-old crabs turn easier than four-decade crabs, and six-decade crabs do not turn at all). But hey, if you can't make the flip on your own, don't get "crabby," just yell for help sooner rather than later, like immediately.

Suggest that all crabs, particularly older crabs with rigid exo-skeletons, do some stretching before attempting any yoga-like speed work.

Como Está Usted

An Ice Breaker with international flair.

■ Play

Stand shoulder to shoulder in a curved line in such a way that the players standing at the ends of the line are touching shoulders also. Well done, that's called a circle.

You need an IT. Got one? Good!

The IT walks around the outside of the circle, eventually stopping to tap one of the circled players on the shoulder. The tapped player turns to face the IT.

The IT bows slightly and says "Buenos Dias." The tapped player, taking their time responding, replies in kind, "Buenos Dias." At which juncture both players spin around and immediately begin walking in opposite directions around the circle until they meet one another, usually about half-way through the walk.

All forward motion must stop (they cannot pass one another—yet) as they shake hands and alternately share the following Spanish greeting: the IT says, "Como está usted," the tapped player responds, "Muy bien, gracias." Both players again bow slightly as they shake hands. This must

be done three times before the players are allowed to
disengage and continue rapidly walking in the direction they
arrived.

The walkers continue around the circle with the first player
back to the gap filling it, leaving the stranded IT to continue
the game by tapping someone new on the shoulder, initiat-
ing a new series of greetings and fast walking. (Be strict
about the walking rule.)

Just one more thing...

Consider the gamesmanship involved in this "muy bien" interlude, which can be ultimately controlled by the person making the final response.

You should know that in Spanish "Como está usted" is "How are you?" in English, "Buenos dias" is "Good Morning" and "Muy bien, gracias" is "Very well, thanks."

Before the game begins, spend some time practicing these greetings as a group and then encourage individuals to mill around, shake hands and greet one another en español. Don't be such a stickler on pronunciation that it detracts from the game.

Variation

If the game seems to be well received, substitute similar greetings in another language using the same game format. If you don't know any other greetings in French, Polish, German, etc. ask if there is anyone in the class who can help you. No? Do some research before the next class. This is an old game with a new diversity twist.

Competition Line-Up

About as long as there have been adventure programs people have doing various forms of *Line-Up* (*Silver Bullets* p.163) and just when you thought there couldn't be another variation...there is.

■ Play

Form two teams of equal numbers. ("But, but we have an odd person." We're all a bit odd, so why don't you join in.)

As implied by the title, this is a competition between the two teams (or more if you have large numbers) to see which team can *line up* most quickly according to the criteria given.

In addition to the familiar categories of date of birth, height, etc. Try these:

- number of siblings, living or deceased
- the number of buttons visible on your clothes
- the width of your smile
- shoe size
- length of hair
- thumb length, knuckle to tip

- alphabetically by last letter of last name
- flat footed overhead reach
- favorite food (alphabetically by first letter)
- number of animals in your home

Arrange 10–12 in a group. If you have four or more groups, have them form a square, pentagon etc. to keep everyone in the same proximity and close to the action as you shout out the categories. When a team thinks they've "got it," have them put their arms on their hips and shout, "We've got it." If you have more than two groups allow the others to continue so you'll have a back -up winner in the event the first team is in err, dropping them of course to a runner-up position.

A nice combination of *Quick Line Up* (*QuickSilver*) and Chronological Line-Up (*Silver Bullets*).

Ready…Go !

Tidbit of Simplicity

Our life is frittered away by detail…Simplify, simplify.

—Thoreau

Corporal Golf

Prior to playing this golf-like travesty, rent the movie video *Caddyshack* and play the section when Chevy Chase (Ty Webb) says, "Be the ball." Another sequencing suggestion: Try an activity called *The Compass Walk* (*Silver Bullets,* pg. 176) before attempting *Corporal Golf.*

The germ (virus) of this idea came via a suggestion by Brett and Peter Harris; Greenwich, CT, and a few choice words by Eric Johnson.

■ Play

You're going to need some playing room, so get thee hence to a well-turfed, full-field situation; unless you have a putt-putt variation in mind, then any ole piece-a-property will do. The first tee should be somewhere on the verge of the field. (The verge and the OB marker in this case are identical.) If you don't understand that last parenthetical reference, no worries, your handicap is secure.

This corporal experience is performed as a threesome. (That's golf talk for 3 people). One of the threesome puts on a blindfold and commits to be the ball. The blindfold should be put on before the threesome approaches the first tee.

- Player #2 is the driver, and wears an intermittent blindfold.

- Player #3 acts as a USGA golf official, who's responsibility it is to create each hole, monitor safety and enforce proper play. The official does NOT wear a blindfold.

- Player #1 (already blindfolded and compassionately led to the first tee) awaits instructions from the driver (player #2).

- The driver looks down the field toward the first hole. (Each hole is conceptualized and passed on to the driver by player #3.) In this case, the hole is represented by the trunk of a large white pine tree approximately 150 yards away, with a dog-leg left around a drinking fountain.

- The driver eyeballs the distance, then tells the ball about how many steps to take, and in what direction. The driver may talk to the ball in great detail, (unless the official calls delay of game), but after the ball starts moving, nothing more may be verbally shared.

- Before the ball moves out, the driver puts on their own blindfold, makes contact with the ball, and the ball/driver combination begin walking in the direction of the hole. The eyes-open official also joins in the walk, now operating as a safety factor, (keeping the ball and driver out of bunkers, etc.) The ball and the driver, while walking down the fairway together, cannot verbally connect, but can respond to each other physically.

- When the ball thinks they have completed what the driver suggested at the tee, all motion stops.

Corporal Golf

> The ball, onced stoped, cannot start up again;
> that's it until the next "shot" is taken. Stopping is
> the signal for the driver to take off their blindfold
> and get ready for the next shot toward the goal,
> essentially repeating what occurred at the tee.

This talk/walk continues until the ball makes physical
contact with the hole. The USGA official must say something definitive (like, STOP!) if it looks like either the ball
or the driver are in jeopardy.

The ball/driver/official roles can be changed after the
completion of each hole. Discussion about roles, function
and cooperation among the three participants can also take
place during this time.

Just one more thing...

The official should take into consideration some of the
natural obstacles, on or around the field, that would make a
hole more challenging or exciting. Consider dog legs, water
hazards, OB areas and bunkers.

After conceptualizing a hole, the official should pass along
distance and geographical instructions to the driver so that
the ball cannot hear what is being shared.

Corporal Golf was not designed to be used in a win/lose
context—unless a decent amount of loose change is
involved.

Cyclops Tag

Leave it to Greek mythology and Tom Quimby, PA Trainer and Plymouth State College professor, to provide a light-hearted comical variation to a classic tag game.

You remember *Pairs Tag or Pairs Squared* (*Cowstails & Cobras II* and *QuickSilver*), those delightful tag games where you're chasing your partner, amongst a mingling milieu of

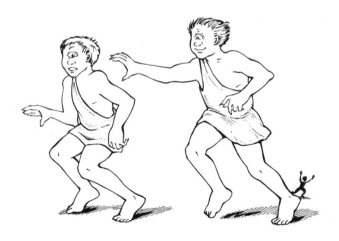

Cyclops Tag

other partners chasing their partners. (The mayhem award for this game goes to the Marblehead Middle School, Marblehead, MA where over two hundred students played it in the school cafeteria. How did it go? Don't ask!)

Mayhem aside...

Remember Homer? Remember the *Iliad* and the *Odyssey*? Then you certainly must remember the Cyclops. They were the giant, monocular creatures featured in these Greek classics. As if their size wasn't intimidating enough, they had a single round eye stuck smack in the middle of their forehead. (The better to see you with my dear!) A Cyclops' role in life was to periodically wreak havoc on other characters featured in these stories. Most epics wreak major havoc as a part of the plot, so these creatures were a classic case of type-casted wreakers.

Mythology aside, here's the variation of *Pairs Tag*.

■ Play

Form a loose fist and hold it up to your eye forming a digital "telescope". You're now looking down the tube of your very own monocular scope. Take your telescoped fist and reduce the size of your scope as seems appropriate to the trust level of your group. The smaller the size of the orifice, the greater the trust level needed.

Close your other eye and use your free hand as a tagging mechanism and as a bumpers-up protection.

Ready.... GO. Determine who's IT and chase or run from your partner using only your Cyclops-like vision to guide you amongst the sea of chaos around you.

Photo Courtesy of Vermont Academy

Where are you during this one-eyed melee? Get in the midst of the playing area and keep a close watch on the scope and extent of the action. This game can get easily out of hand with a young or highly competitive group.

As you run about, envision violently stormy seas and frequently quote from Homer:

> "The son of Zeus spoke, and nodded with his darkish brows, and immortal locks fell forward from the lord's deathless head, and he made great Olympus tremble."

> —*The Iliad*

Okay, okay, quoting from Homer is not that easy, but at least think like a Greek and laugh like a Roman.

Sequence this game well and emphasize compassionate play... or else.

Deeply Rooted

If you're into mind over matter, this is for you. If you're into matter over mind, turn to page 31. This is one of those exercises in which you get to practice concentrating and experience a rather mystifying sensation. This only happens, of course, if you do it correctly, so get into your best concentrating mode and get ready to be mystified.

▇ Play

Everyone needs two partners, so have players find two other folks who were born in different months. Once in threesomes, one player in each group stands firmly upright with their hands by their sides, arms rigid, elbows locked and fists clenched.

The object is for the other partners to stand on either side of their rigid partner and lift them off the ground. Make this first attempt (there will be two) with little preparation other than giving the group a "ready lift" signal.

Lifters do their lifting by grabbing underneath the stiff's clenched fists. Unless sizes and weights are unduly skewed (in which case you should partner up according to similarities in size rather than birth months) this first attempt should be a piece-o-cake in that the lifters experience little problem in getting the liftees a few inches off the ground.

Deeply Rooted

Ready for the mystical part?

Prior to the second attempt, instruct liftees to *get centered*. (That's 1960's talk for get your life in order.) No time for that in these fast paced 90's? Well, at least get the liftees temporarily *rooted*. Seriously, take a moment to concentrate. Ask the lifting partners to be silent. Liftees close their eyes and begin to think of themselves as truly being rooted into the floor/ground. "Focus on your entire body mass being firmly anchored and centered in your mid-section. Imagine that you are a solid and fixed point. Imagine that you are *deeply rooted*." When you feel that you've got it, a nod of the head is the signal for the lifters to once again try to raise their now centered partner off the floor.

Ready, ummph!

If all goes according to plan, they will NOT BE MOVED! How can this be? Is it magic? Is it a higher power? No, it's mind over matter. Now switch roles. Have players trade places and give others a chance to be deeply rooted.

Wait a minute, it didn't work, you got lifted off the ground on both attempts. That's definitely a problem because you know what the opposite of *deeply rooted* is… *shallow*. Oh no, not you, there must be some mistake. OK, OK, you can try it one more time but THIS TIME make sure you REALLY CONCENTRATE !

Thanks to Tim Churchard, PA Trainer, UNH professor and a deeply rooted guy himself for this idea, which he shared at a PA staff training some years ago. Tim didn't even move on the first attempt. Is that rooted or what!

Figaro,* Figaro, Figaro!

"**W**hat's in a name? that which we call a rose,

By any other name would smell as sweet;

So Romeo would, were he not Romeo called,

Retain that dear perfection which he owes, without

that title."

—*Romeo & Juliet*

After some initial Ice Breakers that have successfully broken *the ice* (that is how they got their name you know), try out this little name reminder activity.

▪ Play

Have participants begin to mill about. As the milling begins, suggest they introduce themselves to one another using the phrase, "My name is _____!"

The scene should be reminiscent of a cocktail party gathering. However, unlike the name game of that title (*Cowstails and Cobras*, circa 1976), in which folks simply introduce themselves to one another in a rather conventional

* Figaro—Juliet's Cocker Spaniel

Figaro, Figaro, Figaro!

manner, up the theatrical ante a bit by introducing some spontaneous histrionics. As folks are milling about, simply yell out the manner in which you want them to introduce themselves. For example, as:

...a famous opera singer (Pavoratti would be nice)

...someone very timid and shy

...a very frightened individual

...a smiling (but full of it) car salesman

...someone with great warmth and empathy

...a military commander

...a famous country and western singer

...a suspicious parent (first date)

Figaro, Figaro, Figaro!

Pure fun and pure hilarity—and folks may even learn a few more names. This one could make the top ten list or "my name is not _____!"

Note: To witness a most spirited presentation of this activity visit adventure extrordinaire, Craig Dobkin, at the annual T.E.A.M. Conference in Chicago, Illinois. Craig is co-chair of Play for Peace an international effort sponsored by A.E.E. to introduce play situations to children of conflicting cultures. Nice job, Craig!

Tidbit of Simplicity

Simplicity...
Whose nature is so far
from doing harm,
that he suspects none.

—Shakespeare

Fun-Con-Nada

No props. No time. No ideas. No group. Forget it. But *Fun-Con-Nada* doesn't require much, just a willing group and this suggestion, originally offered years ago by Sarah Smeltzer, of Hartwick College in NY. It's another one to get the creativity flowing.

■ Play

Stand in a non-verbal circle with you included. As initial leader, mime an object with characteristic shape and weight and explain (the circle isn't non-verbal yet) that the fanciful fabricated object is to be passed around the circle twice. If you have encircled 50 people, break it up into five smaller circles... and why are you working with so many people?

As players receive the mimed object, they can change it in whatever creative way they please, as long as it does not involve adding a sound. If someone chooses to pass, respect their choice. That manifest respect further bolsters the validity of Challenge By Choice.

Encourage histrionics and imagination. If you receive an imagined tennis ball from someone (bor-ing!) change it into a histoplasmic goregodulator with automatic drool inhibitor. This exercise is not being graded, so go for the fun and enjoy one another's antics.

Variation

As the amorphous article is passed from person to person, each player makes up a fanciful story (a prevarication, if you will) about the present state of the object. Do not go around this story-telling circle twice, or you may end up with a mimed mutiny. (If you shoot a mime, do you need a silencer?)

Tidbits of Simplicity

★ ★ ★ ★

INVENTIONS

Velcro
(design idea came from sticky burrs)

The Clothespin

Zippers

Post Its

Ball Point Pen

Glass

Bottle cap

Handles

Nails

Go To and Touch Blue

This is actually a combination of two propless games that cause players to think and react quickly. Yeah, but why would somebody want to do that? Jeez, I don't know… it's just a game.

Go To and Touch Blue

■ Play

Cluster a group (This is a game for kids; you define kids.) in the center of a gym and tell them you are going to declare a destination, immediately after which each person is to move with dispatch to that geographical location. Have in

mind a number of obvious and not-so-obvious places to run to. It detracts a lot from the activity if it isn't active; i.e., don't stand there thinking about destinations. Spend some time before class thinking about challenging places to send the kids (not home; be serious), or provide some simple obstacles along the way.

Shout out the destinations with confidence and in such a rapid fire way that the students don't have time to catch their breath or wonder why they are having such a good time doing something that has no tangible purpose.

Go To and Touch Blue

(You want to talk tangible—why are billions of dollars spent annually by millions of people trying to repetitiously put small dimpled balls in holes in the ground?)

That's phase one and can be used as a stand-alone activity. Phase two has to do with what goes on after the players reach a destination.

To double the fun, when you announce a destination, include instructions about a task they must individually achieve when they get there. Touch something blue. Touch leather. Touch a piece of metal jewelry. Touch wood. Or more sensitively, touch someone else's finger, hair, waist— that's it, that's far enough. Notwithstanding the SNAP* factor within the group, touching can easily cross the line and that's the line of no return. You like teaching? Beware who touches what.

Phase two is also a stand-alone activity but as represented by the old Doublemint gum advert, "Double your pleasure, double your fun."

* Sensitive New Age Person

Great to
See You

Think of a time when you thought you saw someone you knew and as you approached them, eyes wide open, smile on your face, hand extended, you suddenly realized that it was not the person you thought it was.

Aaagh... you bob, you weave you do whatever is necessary to save yourself from the embarrassment of enthusiastically greeting a total stranger.

■ Play

Ask a group of 10–20 players to find a partner. Find someone who appears to be about as smart as you are. (If they choose you how smart can they be?)

Have the whole group mill about (sort of a crowd scene) with each partner approximately twenty five feet from one another. Then begin to move very slowly toward one another, all the while waving, smiling, blowing kisses or whatever other motion might indicate a homecoming about to happen. When you get within a few feet of your partner, you realize that this is a TOTAL STRANGER.

What now? Gotta look cool, save face and look dignified.

The obvious solution is simply that you were *really* looking at someone just beyond your partner. So... move right past

Great To See You

your partner without missing a beat, until you make eye contact with your next long lost friend.

But this time, actually greet the person with a hearty handshake or hug, saying the words, "Great to See You!." "Really, Great to See You!"

After the most hearty of greetings, begin again to scan the crowd for yet other lost loves, partners, friends; but now it's back to the original almost enthusiastic but misplaced greeting with the STRANGER.

Use this activity as an ice breaker/get to know you kind of thing, alternating the greetings between the walk by, "I thought I knew you," to the, "Great to See You," real thing, allowing folks to meet and learn names.

Aren't reunions fun?

Grouplets

This activity reads so simply there's a temptation to turn the page looking for something with more play substance, but wait…remember *Pairs Tag?* That quirky/quicky game didn't read well either, but it's a definite winner by all accounts.

■ Play

Ask two people to grasp hands (don't say, "Hold hands," that sounds too permanent and touchy for most middle school students). Before they have a chance to get sweaty palms say, "Now find two different people and form a hand-held triplet." Whoever is left out of the quickly formed troika is OUT OF THE GAME. Continue with, "Gimmie groups of five." Again, whoever is left without a group is also out of the game. Keep announcing different sized groups until almost everyone has been eliminated.

Then what? I don't know, it's your group.

Is it lunch time yet?

Have You Never...?

Many Adventure educators use a get-to-know-you activity called *Have You Ever...?* It involves asking a series of questions prefaced by the words, "Have you ever..." followed by words that depict something revealing. (See *The Bottomless Bag Again!?*, pp. 127–139 for a list of over 500 Have You Evers... and how to use them.)

Here's a tweak on that theme.

■ Play

The idea is to ask a question that reveals if anyone in the group has *never* done something that is considered commonplace. Answer the following and see where you stand — I'm not sure measured against what, but I'll let you work that out. Have you never...

> ...watched an entire VCR movie?
> ...flown in an airplane?
> ...left the state that you were born in?
> ...left the continental United States?
> ...worn sneakers with Velcro, not laces?
> ...played Monopoly?
> ...thrown a Frisbee?
> ...mowed a lawn?
> ...broken a bone?
> ...changed an car tire by yourself?

...gotten a speeding ticket?
...operated a microwave oven?
...eaten a bagel?
...rappelled?
...used a computer?
...eaten tofu?
...used an ATM card?
...set off a fire cracker?
...run a mile without stopping?
...taken a city bus?
...grown zucchini or lived with someone who did?
...eaten at MacDonalds?
...used a circular dial telephone?
...ridden a bike with gears that shift?
...purchased your own underwear?
...programmed a VCR?
...been in an auto accident?
...eaten a Twinkie?
...surfed the net?
...had stitches?
...drunk coffee?
...worn Teva-type sandals?
...taken a black and white photograph?
...watched a black and white TV program?
...played with Silly Putty?
...used an obscenity?
...cleaned a toilet?
...driven a standard shift vehicle?
...sucked your thumb?
...worn a watch?
...eaten an Oreo?
...had a Coca-Cola?
...ridden a two-runner sled?

Humpty Histrionics

This exercise is not a first-day activity. "Performing" in front of your peers requires a sizable chunk of trust. But at the right place and time, Humpty is a zinger.

Remember this ditty?

Humpty Dumpty sat on a wall

Humpty Dumpty had a great fall

All the King's horses and all the King's men

Couldn't put Humpty together again.

■ Play

Recite the ditty and ask players to relate the post-trauma scenario of the fabled accident above as if they were:

> ...a family member of Humpty
> ...reporting the injury to a police detective
> ...the King
> ...one of the King's men
> ...a tabloid news reporter
> ...Humpty's ex-wife
> ...any character that adds to the fun

Humpty Histrionics

Allow a few minutes for volunteers to develop their characters. Don't expect a professionally performed act, encourage participation.

In keeping with the excess of the moment, each performance should receive a rousing standing ovation.

Just one more thing...

Put yourself on the line and do one of the characters, going out of your way to demonstrate the theatrical aspect of the story and how your character humorously relates to the comic tragedy. As you present your character, don't look too good. Flub a line, miss a cue, be the brunt of some good natured laughter. Demonstrate what *laughing with* rather than *laughing at* means. Let players know that the enjoyment factor of the exercise is more significant than individual thespian attempts.

Variation

Set up a multi-character scenario that requires improvisational give and take. Thanks to John Everest for this dandy of an idea.

Tidbit of Simplicity

★ ★ ★ ★

Less is more !

—Unknown

I'm Going on a Trip

This is one of those games that involves the leader saying they are going on a trip and taking a ____. Anyone who wants to join in on the trip must take something that meets the leader's approval. The crux of the game is discovering what criteria the leader has set to allow players to join the select group. Other games of this genre are *Johnny, Johnny…*, *Bugs in My Cup* and *Polar Bears Around the Ice Hole*.

■ Play

In this case the leader says, "I'm going to (any city, or country), and I'll take along anyone who brings the proper clothing." The leader then describes in detail the clothing they are going to take and announces that their chosen, personal wardrobe is perfect. Then it's up to the players to guess what kind of clothes to bring.

The game continues until it's obviously no fun anymore for the people who are having trouble deciding on the proper clothing. Remember, games like this are fun only for the people who have figured out what's going on.

The solution key for this game is to choose the clothes from the waist up that the person to the leader's right is wearing and the clothes from the waist down of the person immediately to the leader's left. Simple? So's yesterday's lottery number.

I'm Going on a Trip

Why play games like this if some people aren't having fun?

- To point out that participants in a group, struggling to come up with a solution to a problem, are wont to continue thinking in the same direction (vertical thinking) rather than channeling their efforts in a more diverse pattern (lateral thinking).

- People in our society form cliques—it happens. People in those cliques often share information not available to those operating at the periphery of the group. That's called, "being in the know." People not privy to the "insiders" knowledge often feel left-out and angry. These "what's the key" games allow players to experience those left-out feelings in a controlled situation.

Considering the above, don't play more than a couple of these games in succession. Someone might not figure out the gimmick for two, three or four of the games you have chosen and begin to have negative feelings about their personal ability to solve problems.

Tidbit of Simplicity

★ ★ ★ ★

Imagination is more important than knowledge.

—Einstein

Map
Making

Want to test your group's observation skills? Try this.

■ Play

The leader takes a stick and draws a circle in the dirt/sand to represent the earth and then says, "Navigation around the globe is made easier by knowing your longitude and latitude" concurrently scratching vertical and horizontal lines within the circle that roughly approximate these navigational lines. (Don't get compulsive about making these lines geographically accurate.)

The leader indicates that anyone in the group can join in a fabulous round-the-earth trip if they can duplicate what the leader just did with the stick. The stick is then passed to a volunteer and an attempt is made.

By this time, you have probably guessed that whatever has been drawn in the dirt is not important and has nothing to do with your tour group entré. Acceptance is entirely dependent upon passing the stick from one hand to the other (after scratching around in the dirt) before passing it along to the next volunteer.

Me Too aka The Chosen Few

Here's another to test those observation skills.

■ Play

Everyone sits on the gym floor or on a dry grassy surface, either in a circle or loose cluster. One person (IT, if you will) volunteers to stand, making themselves obvious as the IT.

IT carefully checks out all the seated folks, making sure not to overlook anyone, then begins choosing different people, asking them to stand in place. When the choosing is completed, the people remaining seated must try to determine what the standing people have in common that caused them to be chosen. The person who guesses first becomes the next IT.

Recognize that the common trait does not have to be visible (only children, members of the glee club…).

Just one more thing…

If you want the game to move swiftly, let the seated people guess out loud what they think the common trait is. A more controlled game has the seated people raise their hand to be recognized by the IT before making guesses.

Name of the Game

This is one of those a-person-leaves-the-room-and-everyone-else-clues-into-what's-happening game, leaving the out-of-room person without a clue. I don't mean to begin on a negative note, but it's important that you recognize the *downer* implications of me-against-the-world type of games; i.e., the possibility of alienating the lone person who's trying to figure out what's going on. If the level of group trust is high, go for it; if you are operating at a developing stage of trust, this game might be utilized better at a later time. Caveats aside, here's the set up for a useful trust building, no prop game that emphasizes cooperation, thinking on your feet and good natured humor.

■ Play

Locate the group in a room that allows seating for everyone and some space for moving around.

Indicate that one or two people will be asked to leave the room. While the volunteers are outside the room, the remainder of the group decides on a subtly repetitive sequence that can be de-coded through answering questions and/or offering a demonstration. The person (people) outside the room are then asked to come back in and try to figure out the pattern; i.e., What's the name of the game?

Name of the Game

The group will probably need some ideas, such as the following, to stimulate their thinking in a useful direction.

Someone in the group begins with a sentence that starts with an A word. For example, "Although what I'm saying may seem strange, the next comment may help." The second comment (from a different person) starts with a B word. "Better listen carefully." The next sentence, offered spontaneously, starts with a C word, and the comments continue, following the alphabet until the contestants figure out what's going on, or the letter Z is reached and the game ends.

Or you might try:

Alternating male and female players as those answering each question. Obviously then, the answers need have no relevance to the questions, as only the alternating of male or female speaker is significant.

Including in each answer the name of a prominent article in the room.

Answering "Yes" to the first question. Thereafter, answer the previous question. Example:

> What day is it?
> **Yes.**
>
> Well, what is your name?
> **Wednesday.**
>
> Are you feeling OK?
> **Arthur.**
>
> Are we playing a game?
> **Just fine.**

Name Roulette

Ever get to a workshop venue and discover that you forgot your *Peek-A-Who* blanket? If that has happened to you, you'll be pleased with this no prop (no blanket) variation that Lee Gillis passed along to me. (Actually, Dr. Lee and a group he was working with at Georgia College and State University serendipitously created the game because Lee forgot his official green, PA *Peek-A-Who* blanket.)

You're wondering what a *Peek-A-Who* blanket is? Check out *Bottomless Bag Again!?* Not fair, not fair... OK, OK... here's a quick reminder, but if you want the whole presentation, including a dandy discourse on rationale, check out the *BBA!?* write up.

Two people (usually instructors) hold up a large blanket or opaque sheet (aka *Peek-A-Who* blanket) so that it forms a sight barrier between two equally-numbered groups hunkered down on either side. When this barrier is dropped (1–2–3 DROP!), two designated people, who are essentially trying to stare through the blanket, try to name each other ASAP. The person who says the other person's name first "wins" that person for their team. There's more, but you'll have to look it up.

Name Roulette

■ Play

Here's the propless version. Divide your group into two smaller groups and ask each grouplet to form a circle. (If there's only 3–4 people in each group, forget it. Sorry I got you into this.) The individuals should be facing the center of their circle. Juxtapose the circles. (If you think about it, there's only one way to juxtapose exterior circles, but paradoxically also an infinite number of ways. If you don't want to think about it, don't bother, it was just something…)

When you say GO, the two circles begin to rotate in opposite directions, either clockwise or counterclockwise. Decide on direction before you say GO. When you say STOP, two people (one in each circle) will be standing back to back. When you say LOOK, those two people spin a one-eighty, and the first of the pair to name the other person wins that person for their circle. Neat, huh?

Just one more thing...

Try using a quick on-and-off boom box to provide the START and STOP aspect of the game. You know, like when you used to play musical chairs. Ravel's Bolero might work well… and maybe not.

Out of Kilter

You'll need a partner for this one so look for someone who appears to be totally opposite of you. Once you've found the antithetical you share what appeared to be most opposite. Be nice, this is no time to make an enemy.

This is an activity about balance, yours' and that of your partner. The object is to always be unbalanced (physically... not mentally).

Play

Grab one another's hands or wrists. Lean backwards until you find that if it were not for the support of your partner, you'd topple over. Of course while you're in the process of putting yourself out of balance your partner is doing the same. Move around a bit and try different positions, all the while maintaining a sense of balance, er...imbalance. As you get more comfortable with one another get a bit more daring. Try a move you couldn't possibly do without the support of your partner.

Ah...you've done it, poetry in motion; Torville and Dean ice dancing, Fred Astaire and Ginger Rogers in the ballroom, Nureyev and Fonteyn performing the Nutcracker.

Now find another pair and make your duo a fourple. Careful, four unbalanced people can lead to a crescendo of falling bodies. Again, the task is to create a point of imbalance that won't work without the support of your partners. When you've mastered four balanced bodies, you're ready for the big one.

Get the whole group together and create one massive example of "human imbalance." Uh....better make sure there's no objects around to fall into or onto, four or more unbalanced bodies are bound to create a bit of havoc.

Tidbit of Simplicity

★ ★ ★ ★

It's really quite simple.

—Richard Harding
(PA's computer wizard
explaining complicated tasks
to the PA staff)

Pairing Up Ideas

Finding a partner is always infinitely more fun when you do something other than, "Alright you guys, count off—one, two, one, two…"

Here are some more ideas for your repertoire:

- Put your right thumb or your left pinky in the air. Find someone displaying the same digit as you.

- Decide if you're an "either" or an "or" person. Label yourself appropriately and then find a partner who is opposite.

- Think of your birthday date (day of the month) find someone so that when you add your dates together, you get an even number.

- Put from 0–5 fingers in the air, find a partner that gives you an odd total.

- Hop on either your left or right foot, find someone who's hopping like you (same foot).

- Find a partner whose favorite movie is different than yours.

- Find someone with a different eye color.

- Find someone with the same thumb size. (or close to it)

- Find someone who appears to be totally opposite from you.

- Find someone who has a different favorite food.

- Find someone wearing a belt, if you are, or someone not wearing a belt, if you aren't.

- Are you a hockey puck or a hockey stick? Pucks go with pucks, sticks with sticks.

- Close your left or your right eye, find someone with the same eye closed as you.

- Find someone who appears to be about as smart as you are.

- Find someone whose tone of voice is similar to yours.

- Find someone whose color of clothing matches yours.

- Are you wearing shoelaces? If so, find someone else who is, if not, find someone who isn't.

- Find someone with a different number of siblings than you.

Tidbit of Simplicity

If it's really that simple wouldn't I know it by now?

—J. Grout
(responding to
Richard Harding's comment)

Phizz, Splot, Grooby

A cognitively stimulating variation of the game, *Count Off*. (*Bottomless Bag* page 95)

The last two times I've played *Count Off* with a group, they accomplished the task on the first attempt, the task being to have a group (eyes closed) of approximately ten people count to twenty without pre-planning or communicating and do this without having two (or more) people say the same number at the same time. Any numbers said simultaneously require a restart at one.

If you have ever been facilitating when a group sails from 1–20 without a hitch, you know the feeling when the group looks at you and says, "That was easy, what's next?"

```
1...2...3...4...5...6...7...8...9...10...11
12...13...14...15...16...17...18...19...20
1...2...?...4...5...?...7...8...9...10...11
12...??...14...15...??...17...18...19...20
1...2...?...4...5...?...7...8...9...10...11
12...??...14...15...??...17...18...19...20
```

Phizz, Splot, Grooby

So now, your five minute activity has dissolved suddenly turned into a ten second activity. Help! (Actually, when this happens simply say, "I'll bet you can't do that again." I have never had a group be able to repeat a first time success the second time.)

By adding this simple alteration you can almost be assured that your groups' first attempt will be followed by a second, leaving you some *real* down time to plan your next activity.

Replace the #3 & #13 with the word Phizz, #6 & #16 with the word Splot and the #9 & #19 with the word Grooby.

Ready Go!

One, Two, Phizz, Four, Five, Splot, Six, Seven, Eight, Grooby, Ten, etc.

"Wait a minute, did I hear two Groobies? Start over again!"

Pixillated Proverbs

"**A** duplication of culinary experts causes damage to the finished product"

What's being said here, let me see, let me see, I know… "Too many cooks spoil the broth!"

Having come from a long line of pixiliated thinkers that was easy for me but how about you and your group? Here's an activity to test your skills in the area of Pixillated Proverbs, Annoying Alliterations and Number Nuances. Not feeling so cognitively challenged? Then move on to *Belly Up*. Otherwise here's how to play.

■ Play

Separate your group into smaller groups of five to seven. Situate yourself somewhat apart from the groups. The games' format is like that of FFEACH (*QuickSilver* p.114). The variation being that there is no miming involved, everything is done verbally.

Have one person from each group come to you on a start signal like… er… ah… uh… "Go!" Remember speed is important. Upon their arrival reveal to each separately, one of the three categories, Pixillated Proverbs, Annoying

Pixilated Proverbs

Alliterations or Number Nuances. The instructions for each category are as follows:

Pixillated Proverbs:

The object here is to take a well know proverb (see above) and rephrase it into something unusual which means more or less the same thing. The other players on the team must guess the original proverb when presented with the re-phrased one. For example: "It is highly desirable to survey the terrain before making a rapid motion." OR "Look Before You Leap."

"You knew that didn't you? Good Job!"

Annoying Alliterations:

This time give out a single letter to the group representative. For example, "T." Upon receipt of this letter the group must make a three word phrase that starts with the same letter. In this instance, Three Thirsty Thrushes, would do the trick. Or perhaps you'd prefer, Ten Twisting Tadpoles or Things That Tick or Thirty Titillating Tunes or…Oh, you get the idea, anything goes if its got three similar letters.

Number Nuances:

Using the numbers 1 through 12 the object is for the group to generate a phrase that has a definite association with the number. If the group representative yells out "1," the response could be, "One for the Money,"

"One for the Pot," "One Good Turn Deserves Another," or "One for All and All for One." The number needn't be the first word as long as it is part of the phrase and the phrase emphasizes the number.

Pixilated Proverbs

Well, back to the format of the action. If you aren't familiar with FFEACH or can't recall it, here you go.

As each group rep runs up to you, give out one of the three categories. No particular order, in fact random is best. Keep it moving as it will help keep the pace of the game slightly frantic. Once the team has guessed correctly, another person from the group comes up for a new category. First team to complete a round (every member has run up once) is the winner. They indicate this by immediately sitting down and yelling, "Pixillated Proverb."

As a facilitator it will help to have written list of the categories and their specifics or you'll find yourself tongue tied as frantic players approach you simultaneously.

Remember… A King unlettered is a donkey crowned!

Proverbial Help List

Special Note: Not a bad idea to have these written out on note cards or strips of paper that can be handed to folks as they run to you. Photographic memory folks excluded.

A king unlettered is a donkey crowned.

A scholastically deprived male member of royalty resembles a long eared ungulate adorned with a bizarre golden head covering.

It's a long lane that has no turning.

Show me an extended section of Rte 30 and I'll show you some serious shikains.

A bird in the hand is worth two in the bush.

One aviarian organism surrounded by digits is far more valuable than two such zooids in well leafed shubbery.

Rats leave a sinking ship.

Rodentia domestica have a tendancy to vacate vessels with negative buoyancy.

Don't count your chickens before they hatch.

Refrain from totaling the available fowl in anticipation of their shell shedding.

It is unwise to maintain numerical compilation of any ungestated members of the pullet species

A watched pot never boils.

Holding a stake out over a stove bound container may slow the contents from reaching 212°.

A maintained vigilance over a vessel with an impending tendency to reach an unstable condition can result in nothing.

Hunger is its own sauce.

An excess of HCL in the digestive holding area precludes having to use Ketchup.

Better to be safe than sorry.

Preclude danger for the sake of post recrimination.

A prudent approach is desired in order to ameliorate the necessity to feel a dooming sense of remorse.

A stitch in time saves nine.

A turn of thread around that button will save having to take at least nine stitches later on.

He who hesitates is lost.

An individual who procrastinates is map and compass material.

A vacillating individual can have a tendency to flounder about wandering aimlessly with no hope of discovery and enlightenment

Pixilated Proverbs

A penny saved is a penny earned.

One hundredth of a buck is one thousandth of a ten spot to the good.

The investment minus the interest on the principal equals the investment.

Don't cry over spilled milk.

Don't become lachrymose over an excess of cow juice.

Limit any overwhelming desire to wail uncontrollably because of events that have already occurred.

Seeing is believing.

Retinal reception is a convincing argument toward verification.

There's no fool like an old fool.

Idiocy is particularly well suited to the more venerable amongst us.

People who live in glass houses shouldn't throw stones.

Sapien organisms that abide in silicon domicles are best advised not to propel geologic artifacts.

(People who live in stone houses shouldn't throw glass.)

Never judge a man until you walk a mile in his shoes.

As the negative side of infinity approaches, attempt not to draw definitive conclusions about a male representative of Homo Sapien until you have ambulated 5,280 feet in that particular Homo's quick starts.

Never judge a book by its cover.

As the negative side of infinity approaches, attempt not to draw definitive conclusions concerning paginated word containers by assuming the content is depicted by what's presented on the exterior.

Poignant Pictures

Have you ever imagined what your facial expression looks like in those genuine moments of being startled, excited, angry, frustrated, etc.?

For example, picture you're on the throne (not in England), you turn to reach for the toilet tissue only to find... it's gone! Imagine Candid Camera had captured your no TP expression. Not a pretty picture, eh?

I trust that, without further mental graphic pictorials, you get the idea of what this game is after; poignant pictures of you, as you and a partner simulate life's real moments.

■ Play

Grab a partner and stand back to back. Either partner initiates the action with the phrase, "What do you look like when..." They then fill in the blank... "when your computer crashes?"

After a mutually silent moment of facial preparation, each player half twirls about, poignantly depicting the moment described. Hold your expression long enough to let your partner enjoy the real you and evaluate your potential for future thespian work. Can't keep a straight face and don't care about future work? Simply enjoy a chuckle and move on to round two as this is truly "reaction by choice."

Poignant Pictures

Need some primers? What do you look like when…

- …you first roll out of bed?

- …your boss says your fired?

- …you've slept through your alarm by over an hour?

- …you just drove over the neighbor's cat?

- …the pilot says we're encountering some turbulence?

- …your puppy relieves himself on your living room carpet?

Okay, the warm-up phase is over, now it's time for competitive PP (*Poignant Pictures*).

Either partner announces three possible choices while standing back to back. After a mutually agreed upon signal

Photo Courtesy of Vermont Academy

like GO, partners spin to face one another and this time the goal is to be expressing the same *Poignant Picture.*

No hints, no secret signals just pure mental telepathy at work here. Can you do three in a row? four? The world record of six was accomplished by a couple married for fifty-two years. After fifty-two years they had given up trying to be different and actually looked alike. Golden anniversaries notwithstanding, grab a partner and set your own personal record, then pair up with another couple and see what four of you can accomplish. Imagine a forple accomplishing a threeple! Now that's a world record for *Poignant Pictures* and creative syntaxing!

Thanks to PA Vermont staff member Rhonda Aubry for encouraging this dramatic interlude of an activity.

Tidbit of Simplicity

**Tis the gift to be simple,
tis the gift to be free.**

—Shaker tune

Poseur

This is not so much competition as an exercise in creativity and sharing.

◼ Play

Dyad-up and with your partner decide on a pose that depicts an identifiable situation; i.e., something you can put a name to.

Circle up as dyads and by turns, each pair situates itself in the center of the circle (give yourselves lots of room) and assumes their chosen pose. All the other pairs also assume that pose to the best of their ability, then guess what the pose depicts. The first pair that guesses is greeted with copious applause and an invitation to be the next pair to display their corporal wares.

Emphasize creating and emulating rather than speed.

Robart Tag

Another in the *Pairs Tag/Everybody's IT* genre. Anticipate: fast action, unique body positioning, variable rules, laughter, self-control.

This run-around game was suggested by PA employee Scott Garman. Scott generously indicated that he had heard about *Robart Tag* from another source, long forgotten. Isn't that the name of the occupational game? Remember, gameophiles, "A good idea doesn't care who has it."

Robart Tag

■ Play

Choose a smallish area for play. Size of the play area is
determined by the number of people playing, but the
boundary guideline for all run-around games is, "If you
wanna play, the action's here."

Players filling this vaguely outlined area place one hand
behind their back, palm facing out. A hand, so presented,
represents the OFF BUTTON for the lower half of that
person's body.

Each player's objective is to touch other players' OFF
BUTTON while preventing their own BUTTON from being
touched.

When an OFF BUTTON is touched, the button's owner
removes that hand from behind their back and freezes from
the waist down. That player now has two free hands to use for
touching the BUTTONS of players careless enough to come
within reach. The frozen player is allowed one pivot step.

If any player inadvertently removes their hand (BUTTON)
from behind their back while trying to touch another player's
BUTTON, or while trying to avoid a touch, their BUTTON is
automatically stimulated, resulting in cryogenic suspension of
the lower extremities—they're frozen.

The game is over when the players get tired of pushing each
other's BUTTONS.

Variations

To end a game that is dragging on (make the playing area smaller next time) announce a Verve Surge that allows frozen participants one full step and a pivot.

Two evenly-matched opponents (shuckin' and jivin', but not confrontin') have fifteen seconds (do a verbal count down) to push each other's BUTTON, or the game ends in a tie.

Sweet Harmony

A few years ago I was at an awards ceremony for folks who had contributed significantly to their community in one way or another. It was a rather moving evening as many in the audience stood up and gave testimony to those receiving awards. Just as the evening was about to come to a close, one fellow stood up and said he didn't really have anything to say... but he was so moved by the evening, he wondered if he might offer a song.

He nonchalantly stood up and broke into song, a beautiful ballad. He didn't have a great voice, he was not a singer by trade, but he filled the room with enthusiasm and passion.

Sweet Harmony

Nice story, right? But, you're no doubt wondering what this story has to do with you and this next activity, right? The answer is "everything."

It's a commonly known fact that the number one fear for most people is public speaking, secondly only to, you guessed it, public singing.

Well, this activity gives you the opportunity to be very public with your singing but to do so amidst such bedlam that nary a fear you'll have. Here's how!

■ Play

Encourage the group to generate song titles to which the words are very familiar. You know…Happy Birthday, Take Me Out to the Ball Game, Santa Claus is Coming to Town, Yellow Submarine, The Star Spangled Banner, etc. The more the better.

Then ask folks, upon your command, to pick one tune and begin singing it, like the man at the Awards Ceremony, with enthusiasm and passion. As with the game Categories (*QuickSilver* p.86) have folks group themselves according to the tune they are singing. For example, all the folks singing Take Me Out to the Ball Game would eventually find one another and be singing as one. Take the time to go around and give each group the opportunity to "belt out their tune."

Do a number of rounds, solicit new tunes for the song menu and encourage folks to release their musical inhibitions.

For variations, try whistling and humming or even kazoos. Hey, wait a minute this is a no prop book. Forget the kazoos!

Take Me To Your Leader

Yet another way to instill trust in a group after having followed various prescribed trust sequences previously published in other PA publications. Wow!

More simply put, don't try *Take Me To Your Leader* until your group is displaying a fair amount of trust.

■ Play

Establish an area about the size of half a football field (or use a field already there). Have the members of your group (10+ is good) position themselves randomly from one end of the area to the other. Not too far apart, approximately 15–20 feet between one another.

Have a blindfolded volunteer place themselves at either end of the group. On a signal of "Go" have this person begin, at a comfortable pace and with bumpers up, to attempt to cover the distance between the two end lines, making contact with every person in the area during the journey.

How, you might ask, can one possibly find all the people in the area while blindfolded or with one's eyes hermetically sealed? Easy enough. One simply repeats the command, "Take me to your leader!" and listens carefully for the response, "Follow me!" which should be provided by the

Take Me To Your Leader

next closest person in the continuum of randomly positioned folks between the boundaries.

How do runners know when they have found the leader and completed the circuit? Simple, the last person greets the exhausted, but now trust-filled traveler with the secret handshake that only the "Leader" could possibly know, having once traveled this route as an apprentice.

Just one more thing...

This is a useful trust activity to introduce once you've got your group beyond inappropriate gaminess with one another. The effectiveness of this activity results from the sequenced "blind" movement that occurs from player to player. Proctor this activity well and don't allow any shenanigans from the sighted participants that might reduce whatever trust has been established.

Could you do this for speed and see how quickly a runner could traverse the area safely? Sure, but don't, this is a trust activity. Take me to your leader... c-a-r-e-f-u-l-l-y.

Tic-Tac-Toe —Live!

This is very simple if you know how to play Tic-Tac-Toe (T-T-T), and if you don't, where you been? This game can be strictly recreational or part of the experiential/problem-solving genre of games—your choice.

■ Play

Using some playground chalk (the kind that washes away in a rain), or scratching lines in the dirt, or laying out sections of rope, or taping the gym floor, reproduce the well know T-T-T grid. If you have a lot of people, extend the grid (more squares).

To physically include people in the game, use them as T-T-T pawns. To designate yourself, it's hands on your head for an O, or cross arms over your chest for an X. Three congruent folks in a row designates a winner, no ties (CAT games) allowed—unless you want to.

As the game begins, players designate themselves as either an X or O and insert themselves into what they think is a potentially winning position. No discussion (or body language) is allowed between players once the game begins. Does this give you any idea of how intense a game scenario can result? Just a rhetorical question, relax.

Just one more thing...

Other than the fun of including yourself in a 3-D version of a classic game, value can result from talking about how the groups (teams?) handle victory and defeat, because T-T-T is blatantly a win/lose situation.

How is the remainder of the team going to react to another player positioning him or herself poorly?

Try playing the game but allowing discussion between team members before moves are made. Whether to allow pre-game discussion depends upon how much review material you are looking for in a post-game debrief.

Tidbit of Simplicity

Spartan simplicity must be observed. Nothing will be done merely because it contributes to beauty, convenience, comfort, or prestige.

—From the Office of the
Chief SignalOfficer,
US Army, May 1945

Weird Walkin'

Activities don't get much simpler than this. Thanks to that very diverse guy Bart Crawford for simply passing it along. Practical results and aesthetic considerations are of less concern than unselfconscious, off-the-wall participation. Be open to the bonding potency of *shared stupidity*.

◼ Play

Assemble your group anywhere. The only criteria for this existential gathering place is that from "anywhere" the players need to be able to walk unencumbered in a fairly straight line for approximately fifty feet.

Ask each player, as it fits their volunteerism and sense of chutzpah, to walk toward that fifty-foot distant destination, displaying as they walk some affectation or histrionic display of spontaneous creativity. Remember Monty Python's Ministry of Weird Walking—like that. Each player is allowed ample time to display their peculiar weird walk, with supportive cheers produced in stereo from both ends of the walking venue.

When all have completed their individual walk (with a viewed sense of palpable relief), ask for pairs to create a weird walk in tandem. Then triplets, then... as a finale, the entire group combines their creative efforts toward an en mass ambulation of spectacular proportion, followed by copious applause and untethered smiles.

Tidbits of Simplicity

CHILDREN

Some time ago I was working with a kindergarten class as a favor to a friend. I like little ones well enough but am challenged as to how to get their attention. I was having a successful morning with them and even had their rapt attention on most occasions (or thought I did). After carefully explaining the rules to our final activity, I wanted to make certain that everyone one was clear about what we were about to do. (Although I must admit the attentive looks on their cute faces convinced me their understanding was total). So I asked, "Does anyone have any questions?" A spunky little guy in the front row threw up his arm and said; "DO YOU HAVE ANY M & M'S?"

Moral: Just when you think it needs to be complex...it doesn't !

—Karl Rohnke

Welded Ankles

"**D**ifficulty is in the eyes (ankles) of the beholder."

■ Play

Ask a group of fifteen or so players to stand shoulder to shoulder and make conscious contact with each other's ankles; i.e., stand ankle to ankle with the person next to you. The challenge is to try, as a group, to move fifteen feet forward (place a rope on the ground as a goal) without losing physical contact with each other's ankles.

This is harder than it looks (sounds), so make enough time available to allow more than a couple attempts. If fifteen minutes have gone by without completion of the fifteen feet, announce that the group has just two attempts remaining. This restriction will either cause the group to focus and complete the distance skin-to-skin, so to speak, or allow the group to judiciously fail and be availed of that famous facilitation query, "Considering that you didn't complete the announced distance, do you consider what you just did success or failure?" Well, what do *you* think?

There's obviously variables as to what the answer can or should be, but the words *failing forward* come to mind. Take it from there oh verbal one, but make your point with a feathered brush lest a sledge hammer destroy the lesson.

If you have multiple groups of 10–15 trying to accomplish this task, when a group succeeds suggest that they disperse and try to help other groups succeed also; gives you something to talk about; makes people feel good, too.

Wham Sam Sam

Sometimes the silliest things are the most useful. Thanks to Sandy Sheppard, University of Buffalo, for passing on this bit of spontaneous buffoonery. Experience will tell you when a silly game is right or wrong, which isn't going to help you much right now, so be conservative and hold *Wham Sam Sam* for a future time if you think your group isn't ready—though they probably are.

■ Play

Get five to fifty people standing in a circle. Ask these circular standees to listen to what you say and watch what you demonstrate, because after a couple practice attempts, it's-a-happening. Say and do the following with gusto, this is no time to be apologetically playful.

Say "Wham Sam Sam" and at the same time bend over and slap the person's knees (just above the knees actually) to your right. Slap (be compassionate) three times, concurrent with the exclamation, "Wham Sam Sam." Do this twice... Wham Sam Sam (slap, slap, slap), Wham Sam Sam (slap, slap, slap).

Say, "Gooey, gooey, gooey, gooey" at the same time that you stroke the chin of the person to your left four times with your right hand (one stroke per gooey); kind of a gentle pinching stroke between thumb and fingers.

Do another Wham Sam Sam.

Raise both arms over your head and make a 360° turn while saying "A Wha Hee," (accent on the Wha). Do it again.

Do the gooey gooey thing again.

Finish up with a repeat of Wham Sam Sam.

Just one more thing...

There are no specific consequences for missing a word or beat, only that hurry-up feeling of being out of sync. The benefits of participation and error are laughter at self and others in a supportive setting. If the laughter is derisive and comments are hurtful, this was the wrong game at the

Wham Sam Sam

wrong time. Remember, many of these activities are best received when presented in a trust-building sequence.

Variation

Speed up the sequence. Reverse the direction. Everyone face away from circle center and Wham Sam Sam.

Project Adventure Services and Publications

■ Services

Project Adventure, Inc. is a national, non-profit corporation dedicated to helping schools, youth groups, camps, corporations, counseling groups, physical education programs and others implement Project Adventure ideas. Characterized by an atmosphere that is fun, supportive and challenging, Project Adventure programs use non-competitive games, group problem-solving Initiatives and ropes course events as the principal activities to help individuals reach their goals; to improve self-esteem, to develop strategies that enhance decision making, and to learn to respect differences within a group. Toward these ends, the following services are available:

Project Adventure Workshops

Through a network of national certified trainers, Project Adventure conducts workshops for teachers, counselors, youth workers, and other professionals who work with people. These workshops are given in various sections of the country. Separate workshops are offered in Project Adventure Games and Initiatives, Challenge Ropes Course Skills, Counseling Theory and Techniques for Adventure Based Programs, and Interdisciplinary Academic Curriculum.

Services and Publications

Challenge Course Design and Installation

Project Adventure has been designing and installing ropes courses (a series of individual and group challenge elements situated indoors in a gymnasium or outdoors in trees) since 1971. PA Staff can travel to your site and design/install a course appropriate for your needs and budget.

Equipment Sales

A catalog service of hard-to-find props, materials and tools used in adventure programs and the installation and use of Challenge Ropes Courses.

Corporate Programs

Management workshops for business people and professionals. These workshops are designed for increasing efficiency of team members in the workplace. The trust, communication, and risk-taking ability learned in these programs translate into a more cohesive and productive team at work.

Program Accreditation

The Accreditation process is an outside review of a program by PA staff. Programs that undertake the accreditation process are seeking outside evaluation with regard to quality and safety. The term accreditation means "formal written confirmation." Programs seeking confirmation are looking to ensure that they are within the current standards of safety and risk management. This assurance may be useful for making changes in program equipment and/or design, and in providing information on program quality to third parties such as administrators, insurance companies and the public.

To Contact Project Adventure

Project Adventure has several overseas offices, including Australia, New Zealand, Japan, Singapore and Taiwan. For further information, contact PA headquarters:

U.S. Offices

Project Adventure, Inc.
P.O. Box 100
Hamilton, MA 01936

TEL: 978/468-7981
FAX: 978/468-7605

Southeast
P.O. Box 2447
Covington, GA 30015

TEL: 770/784-9310
FAX:770/787-7764

West Coast
P.O. Box 14171
Portland, OR 97293

TEL: 503/239-0169
FAX: 503/236-6765

Vermont
P.O.Box 1640
Brattleboro, VT 05302

TEL: 802/254-5054
FAX: 802/254-5182

Services and Publications

■ Publications

If you would like to obtain additional copies of this book, an order form is provided on the next page. Project Adventure also publishes many books in related areas. Described below are some of our best sellers, which can be ordered on the same form. Call or write to Project Adventure for a complete publications list.

QuickSilver

Adventure Games, Initiative Problems, Trust Activities and a Guide to Effective Leadership

This latest offering from cooperative games master Karl Rohnke contains over 150 new games, problem solving initiatives, ice breakers, variations on old standards, trust, closures and more. There is also a section on leadership with co-author, Steve Butler, in which they impart many of the secrets that they use when leading and designing programs.

by Karl Rohnke and Steve Butler

Cowstails and Cobras II

Karl Rohnke's classic guide to games, Initiative problems and Adventure activities. Offering a thorough treatment of Project Adventure's philosophy and approach to group activities, Cowstails II provides both the experienced practitioner and the novice with a unique and valuable resource.

By Karl Rohnke

Services and Publications

Silver Bullets

More Initiative problems, Adventure games and trust activities from Karl Rohnke: 165 great games and activities that require few, if any, props. Use this as a companion to Cowstails and Cobras II or a stand alone guide to invigorate your program.

By Karl Rohnke

Youth Leadership In Action

All too often young people have little access to the resources necessary to improve their skills and develop their leadership potential. Youth Leadership In Action addresses this need by providing a guide for youth leaders to implement experiential, cooperative activities and techniques into their programs.

But the most striking and unique feature of this book is that it was written by a group of youth leaders. This group of eight leaders have taken 54 of Project Adventure's most popular Adventure games and activities and rewritten the instructions and rules in the way they present and play them. They also give a brief history of Project Adventure, present their own definition of Adventure, and explain some of PA's basic concepts and techniques — Full Value Contract, Challenge By Choice, debriefing, sequencing, etc. They also provide a section on effective leadership and how to start several types of programs.

Edited by Steve Fortier

Order Form

Ship to:

Name _____

Address (no P.O. Box nos.) _____

_____

City _____ State _____ Zip _____

Phone (_____) _____ Ext _____

Due to the inability to trace Parcel Post shipments, it is our policy to ship U.S. orders via UPS.
We must have a UPS shipping address (no Post Office box numbers).

Book Rate will be used for orders sent to foreign countries and in cases of insufficient street addresses.

Payment: ❏ Check   ❏ MasterCard   ❏ VISA

Credit Card # _____ Exp. ___ / ___

Signature _____

(Signature required for all charge orders.)

☛ **TO ORDER PLEASE CALL: 800/795-9039   FAX: 978/524-4600**

or return this form to: **Project Adventure, Inc.**
P.O. Box 100
Hamilton, MA 01936

Qty.	Title	ISBN	Cost	Total
	Youth Leadership in Action	0107-3	15.00	
	QuickSilver	0032-8	25.00	
	Silver Bullets	5682-X	22.00	
	Back Pocket Adventure	1419-1	14.00	
	Cowstails II	5434-7	22.00	

* **TAX-EXEMPT** orders must be accompanied by a copy of the purchaser's certificate of tax exemption.

How to Calculate Shipping Charges

- **Add $4.00** for first book.
- **Add .50c** for each additional book up to 5 books.
- **Over 5 books,** add 5% of total.

On books being shipped to AK, HI, Canada and foreign countries:
- 4.50 to Alaska & Hawaii
- 6.50 to Canada
- 7.00 on foreign orders

On orders of 5 or more books, call Project Adventure for exact shipping cost.

Subtotal _____

Please add sales tax:
GA add 6%
VT & MA add 5% _____

Tax Exempt No.* _____

Shipping (instructions at left) _____

TOTAL _____

No Prop Reference List

Silver Bullets

5-5-5- Duo Isometrics	161
Add on Tag	42
Balloon Blow-up	173
Bang Your Dead	54
Basic Killer	52
Body English	35
Bottoms Up	159
Candle	160
Chronological Line-Up	163
Coming & Going of the Rain	93
Commandant	74
Compass Walk	176
Count Coup	78
Count Off	179
Diminishing Load	138
Dizzy Izzy Tag	155
Dog Shake	168
Everybody Up	100
Everybody's It	153
Flip Me The Bird Tag	155
Fried Egg Simulator	174
Front & Back Roll Practice	86
Funny Face	169
Hands Down	53
Hog Call	98
Hop On Tag	155
Human Camera	177
Impulse	34
Inch Worm	158
Invisible Jump Rope	157
Izzat You	76
Knots (Hands Tangle)	117
Marathon Whistle	175
Medley Relay	179
Mini Balance Test	160
Mirror Image	170
Mrs. O'Grady	180
PDQ Test	172
People to People Surfing	146
Popsicle Push-Up	166
Red Baron Stretch	161
Sardines	30
Seat Spin	148
Sherpa Walk	89
Slow Mo	94
Sore Spot Tag	154
Squat Thrust	94
Stork Stretch	162
Tegwar	56
Texas Big Foot	46
The Clock	116
The Monster (Four Pointer)	133
The Ten Member Pyramid	149
Toe Tag	154
Toss- A - Name Game	17
Traffic Jam	122
Triangle Tag	155
Trust Sequence	81
Two by Four	123
Yeah, But	91

Adventures in Peacemaking

Ballooning & Draining	153
Can You Guess	133
Duck & Chicken	110
Humachines	64
Human Bridges	74
If	201
King Frog	165*
Pass the Shoe	56
Pete & Repeat	104
Pick Your Corner	190
Slot Machine	129
Speedy Threesome	161

Into the Classroom

Body Pass	59
Communication Exercise	87
Essences	86
Heirlooms	65
Human Machine	58
Personal	65
The Monster Race	70
Tiny Teach	61

Cowstails & Cobras II

Warm-ups

360 Spin	32
Criss-cross	30
Crow Hop	30
Dance Hopping	32
Duo Hopping	32
Entrechat	31

No Prop Reference List

Cowstails & Cobras II

Warm-ups (continued)

Group Hopping	33
Heel & Toe Touch	32
Heel Clicker	32
Hop & Spin	32
Hop on One Leg	32
Jump & Lift	32
Scissor kick -hop	32
Ski Hopping	30
5-5-5 Duo Stretching	33
Bottoms Up	36
Everybody Up	36
Grab Your Toes	35
Hustle Handle	66
Inch Worm	35
Initiative Run	89
Levitation	53
Python Pentathlon	43
Reach & Grab	35
Red Baron Stretch	34
Return to the Earth	41
Row Boat Stretch	36
Side Bender	33
Speed Rabbit	63
The Angel	33
The Cobra	43
Yelling	45
Yurt Circle	73

QuickSilver

Bumpity Bump Bump	84
Categories	85
Commons	110
FEEACH	114
Have You Ever...?	224
Hog Call	202
Hustle Handle	87
It Ain't Me Babe	80
Knee Slap	246
Name Tag	207
Pairs Squared	90
Remember Gooney	251
The Bends	240
Trust Circle	233
Trust Wave	234
Twizzle	137
Where In the Circle Am I?	92

QuickSilver (continued)

Whizzz Bang	141
Zombie	142

Bottomless Bag Again!

Bang, You're...	45
Blind Fold Line Up	98
Bottoms Up	6
Bumpity Bump Bump	9
Caught Ya Peekin'	125
Count Off	95
Dog Shake	15
Elbow Tag	2
Everybody Up	96
Everybody's It	1
Hands Down	46
Have you ever...?	127
Hospital Tag	2
Human Camera	18
I've Got the Beat	47
Impulse Genre	141
Pairs Tag	2
Passing Xed or UnXed	47
Popsicle Push Up	96
Retro-eknhor	9
Reversing Pyramid	95
Sore Spot Tag	2
Team Tag Tag	4
The Wave	88
Your Add	48

FUNN STUFF 1

Ah So Ko	1
Circle Slap	26
Subway Sardines	47
Whoops Johnny...	108

FUNN STUFF 2

Climb All Over Me	27
Coreolis	38
Gotcha	6
Hut, 2, 3, 4...	21
I'm One Too!	7
Leaning Tower of Feetza	22
Metamorphose	12
Normative Chaos	34
Ring Around the Trust	32
Switcheroo	5
The Button Factory	2
The Spotting Gauntlet	35
Wild, Wild Women	2

FUNN STUFF 3

*The games in Funn Stuff 3 are
soon to be published and, as
such, are not paginated.*

Angle
Clone
Emotions Tag
Group Stretch
One Pa-ta-ta...
Thumbelina
Who're You?

BackPocket Adventure

7-11	23
Air Traffic Controller	25
Back to Back	29
Belly Up	31
Como Está Usted	33
Competition Line-Up	36
Corporal Golf	38
Cyclops Tag	41
Deeply Rooted	44
Figaro, Figaro, Figaro!	47
Fun-Con-Nada	50
Go To and Touch Blue	52
Great to See You	55
Grouplets	57
Have You Never...?	58
Humpty Histrionics	61
I'm Going on a Trip	63
Map Making	65
Me Too	67
Name of the Game	68
Name Roulette	70
Out of Kilter	72
Pairing Up Ideas	74
Phizz, Splot, Grooby	76
Pixillated Proverbs	78
Poignant Pictures	83
Poseur	86
Robart Tag	87
Sweet Harmony	90
Take Me To Your Leader	92
Tic-Tac-Toe—Live!	94
Weird Walkin'	96
Welded Ankles	98
Wham Sam Sam	100